WINTER IS FUN!

by Walt K. Moon

BUMBA BOOKS™

LERNER PUBLICATIONS ◆ MINNEAPOLIS

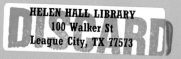

Note to Educators:

Throughout this book, you'll find critical thinking questions. These can be used to engage young readers in thinking critically about the topic and in using the text and photos to do so.

Lerner Publications Company
A division of Lerner Publishing Group, Inc.
241 First Avenue North
Minneapolis, MN 55401 USA

For reading levels and more information, look up this title at www.lernerbooks.com.

Library of Congress Cataloging-in-Publication Data

The Cataloging-in-Publication Data for *Winter Is Fun!* is on file at the Library of Congress.
ISBN 978-1-5124-1410-3 (lib. bdg.)
ISBN 978-1-5124-1535-3 (pbk.)
ISBN 978-1-5124-1536-0 (EB pdf)

Manufactured in the United States of America
1 — VP — 7/15/16

Expand learning beyond the printed book. Download free, complementary educational resources for this book from our website, www.lernerresource.com.

Table of Contents

Winter Season

Each year has four seasons.

Winter is one season.

Temperatures are cold in winter.

Winter comes after fall.

Days are shortest in winter.

The sun rises late.

It sets early.

Snow falls.

Water freezes.

It becomes ice.

Icicles hang.

Why does water turn to ice in winter?

Many plants stop growing.

They cannot live in the cold.

These trees are evergreens.

They keep growing in winter.

They stay green all year.

Many animals grow thick fur.

Fur keeps animals warm.

What do you think happens to the thick fur after winter?

Some animals hibernate.

They find a warm place.

They rest.

They wake up in spring.

Why do you think some animals hibernate in winter?

17

Winter has many holidays.

Some people celebrate Christmas.

Others celebrate Hanukkah.

New Year's Day is on January 1.

People wear warm clothes.

They play in the snow.

They go sledding.

They build snowmen.

What do you do in winter?

Seasons Cycle

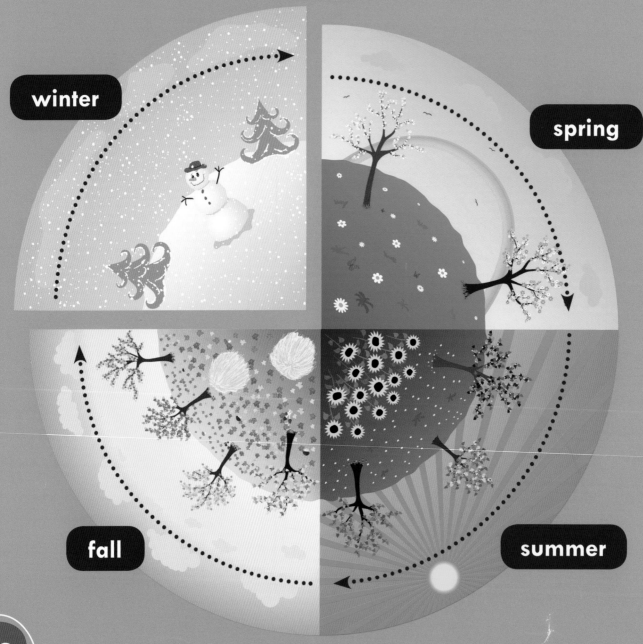

winter

spring

fall

summer

Picture Glossary

evergreens

trees that stay green all year

hibernate

to sleep all winter

icicles

ice that forms from
dripping water

sledding

sliding down
a hill on a sled

23

Index

Read More

Anderson, Sheila. *Are You Ready for Winter?* Minneapolis: Lerner Publications, 2010.

Bix, Jasper. *Dressing for the Cold.* New York: Gareth Stevens Publishing, 2015.

Rice, William B. *The Seasons.* Huntington Beach, CA: Teacher Created Materials, 2015.

Photo Credits